BEWARE MILLIPEDE

Published by
Kachere Series
P.O. Box 1037, Zomba, Malawi

ISBN: 978-99908-87-22-8 (Kachere Books no. 34)

The Kachere Series is represented outside Africa by
African Books Collective, Oxford (orders@africanbookscollective.com)
Michigan State University Press, East Lansing, MI (msupress@msu.edu)

Layout and cover Design: Caroline Chihana

Printed by Lightning Source

Beware Millipede

Zondiwe Mbano

Kachere Books no. 34

Kachere Series
Zomba
2008

Kachere Series
P.O. Box 1037, Zomba, Malawi
kachere@globemw.net
www.kachereseries.org

This book is part of the Kachere Series, a range of books on religion, culture and society from Malawi. Other Kachere books are:

Anthony Nazombe, *Operations and Tears: A New Anthology of Malawian Poetry*

Pia Thielmann, *Hotbeds: Black-White Love in Novels from the United States, Africa and the Caribbean*

Pia Thielmann, *Hotbed: Black and White Love in Novels from the United States, Africa, and the Caribbean*

Hoffman Aipira, *Reflections and Sunsets*

Ernst Wendland, *Sewero: Christian Drama and the Drama of Christianity in Africa*

Kudzai Nhamo, *A Silent Battle*

Joseph Banda, Patrick Kupatsa and Misheck Kathumba, *Behind the Baobab Tree*

Desmond Dudwa Phiri, *Let us Fight for Africa: A Play on the Chilembwe Rising*

Masiye Tembo, *Touched by His Grace. A Ngoni Story of Tragedy and Triumph*

Orison Ian Boma Mkandawire, *Chiswakhata Mkandawire*

The Kachere Series is the publications arm of the Department of Theology and Religious Studies of the University of Malawi

Series Editors: J.C. Chakanza, F.L. Chingota, Klaus Fiedler, P.A. Kalilombe S. Mahommad, Chimwemwe Katumbi

Dedication

For publishing these poems, the editors and staff of Kachere Series deserve my sincere gratitude. I am especially grateful to Dr. Klaus Fiedler, who kept reminding me as I tried to gain time so that I find a few lost poems, and write one or two more; without his constant reminders, the exercise was going to be endless.

I dedicate this collection of my poetry to Wongi, Umsa, and Lunga.

Contents

Beware Millipede

Now that the *msangu* tree
Is bringing forth leaves
Adieu rain, adieu visitor

Now that birds twitter, building
Nests up in the *msangu*
Beware millipede, beware fool

From mountains, rivers run
Fast through dry lands
For waters must hasten to the lake

From above, the sun stares harsh
Over lands scorched brown
And wildfires lick the land to ash

Adieu rain, adieu visitor
You flood rivers and lakes
But fail to fill holes of anthills

Now that the *msangu* towers
In greenery, with nests
Dangling like succulent fruit

Beware fool, beware of the heat
For under the *msangu* are thorns
And the baobab gives no shade

Beware, for October is a furnace
Melting and casting to rings
The metallic glow of your segments

Beware millipede, do not burrow
For bulldozers lift the earth
And grind it between their teeth

Sunset over Mparayi

Now shadows elongate
Reaching towards the lake
That gives birth to the sun

Cattle slowly shuffle
And dust rises high
Like an oblation for rain

Boys riding on cattle
Chant the glory of their bulls
And whistle nostalgic tunes

Girls balancing pots
Yodel wistful songs
Fanning their secret fire

Men shouldering their kill
Cross fields to the idyllic
Welcome of wives and children

Hungry fires on verandas
Lick pots that flavour
The home and absorb fatigue

The sun crowns Mparayi
And drapes ribbons of gold
Over the slopes to Lukonkobe

Behind Mparayi a velvet
Cloud stretches upwards
To welcome home the sun

And now darkness stalks
Children and covers shadows
Skulking around the fires

Matora

The lorry suddenly stops; our hearts
Leap: a rat has run into itching paws!
Where to? the stern voice of the Law:
White-topped cap, long white sleeves
Khaki trousers, and shiny black boots...
Nonchalant look of the driver, like
A toddler picking up a scorpion. DOWN!
DOWN ALL! words of authority. Quickly,
Simple mortals nurtured in obedience - a cobra
Springing from the tarpaulin could not have
Commanded such terror - we all jump off.
Behind the lorry, a shrine for propitiation
(No white cock!). The driver proffers a crumpled
Greenish note (...Promise to pay the bearer...).
Eyes express the Law appeased. A handshake,
A few words, a nod, a smug smile, a beckon to us
A wave of hands, and that's all! Among immortals
Material counts for little; it is the spirit of giving
That pleases them eternally. In the evening:
Packets of madness to wallow in, blaring music
To rouse the animal, and finally staggering into
Dark rooms commissioned to sow the new pox.

Prayer for Rain

Eye of the sky
Staring harsh on us
Wink some times

We are soft clay
Wrought by your hand
Roused by the wind

We are your children
Shrivelling in hot sand
Without water or food

But those wielding the spear
Have mansions flowing with water
And tables cloying with fat

* * *

Remember the long march
Across the forest and rivers
With songs on our lips

The beat of the drum united us
Our fathers' sagely stride led us
To that mountain of promise

Remember those we buried
In the belly of the forest
Brave sons and daughters

Now is this the arriving
Or have we gone roundabout
To the same old shacks

* * *

How do we trace the way
Without torches in the dark
When grey heads talk riddles

They lock the only door
And proclaim to four winds
That we are free to enter

They open the door wide
And have in chains the legs
Of those who dare walk in

Then they loosen the chains
And yet position bulldogs
Snarling from behind the door

* * *

Long before the sun
Dried songs on our lips
We always feared this

For Mbona came to warn of
The blood of lechery and treachery
Dripping on the shrine at Msinja

John Chilembwe organised
Martyrs to spit curses at those
Who prolong *thangata* system

And Levi Mumba pointed
To poisons in cups and bottles
During native tea-parties

* * *

We have always feared this
As tobacco estates deflower
Forests ancient as the rain

12

And elders instruct adolescents
To play touch-and-run in the dark
Following rules in condom packets

Did Napolo not quake mountains
And flush down rocks and water
To sweep away entire villages

Did Vwira not scoop lakes
Across acres of hybrid maize
Down the Lukonkobe and Kasito

* * *

When people burn in a house
Is it an occasion for killing
Escaping rats and cockroaches

Is it an occasion for reminiscing
And pointing spears at those
Who dare bring in hosepipes

In the roasting heat of October
Napolo guzzles the Mulunguzi dry
Sending scholars packing again

When a child grows teeth
Don't you wean him to *sima*
Before he chews your nipples

* * *

Let it rain this year
Rain, so that dust settle
Dust, smelling of tobacco

For Lilongwe is the capital
And dust can shroud vision
Of the extent of this country

From Chitipa with food in plenty
But impossible roads to Nsanje
With no rain but water in plenty

Relentless eye of the sky
Wink and let your eyelids
Rain down tears of pity

Zomba, CC 1992

Rain in Salima

This insistent pattering
On the roof, pattering

All night, weary night
Of no thunder, no sleep

Long night of bats squealing
As they flap about in darkness.

September scorched the land
And October came to bake it

Now November has gone,
Leaving only pattering rains;

This intractable pattering
Long in the dead of night

And swarms of tiny vamps
Singing long silvery tunes

******

I have seen many evenings
Descending from Mparayi

Evenings that emerge stealthily
From holes of chirping insects

Evenings that throw darkness
Over lurid clouds of sunset

Evenings when the new moon
Summons children to play

Lonely evenings of a widow
Haunted by wails of a he-goat

Drowsy evenings that wrap
Heavy days in dead sleep

Dark evenings of owls hooting
From graves: I've seen them all

******

I have seen many mornings
Welcoming a hopeful sun

Mornings that deliver clearly
Distant crows of dutiful cocks

Mornings of the wild dove cooing
From high on the *ciyombo* tree

Serene mornings that radiate
From the hoe of the early farmer

Cold mornings that blow away
Sleep from eyes of the herdsboy

Mornings that spread out
Like a woman in her delivery

Bringing forth the sun to light
The world: I've seen them all

*****

This insistent pattering
Through evening to night

And now darkness has gone
Uncovering a grey morning

A morning of pattering rain
Over land drowned in floods

And now the sight of huts
Isolated like small islands

The sight of huts tumbled down
Into heaps of mud and grass

The sight of grass and shrubs
Laden with insects and crawlers

The sight of folk with bulky loads
On their heads, wading to dry land

The sight of children that spurn
All gloom and play in the water

And the sight of men recovering
Bodies from heaps of mud and grass

*****

I had thought rain comes
To wake seeds from the soil

To cleanse the air of all dust
And make it light and pure

But this rain, pattering all
Night, all day, pattering;

This rain, flooding all rivers
To charge at us from uplands;

Today, this rain persecutes us
This rain comes to destroy us

Lake Kazuni

Lap, lap ripples of Kazuni
Lap against your muddy shore

Lap and listen to the roaring storm
Tearing down the youthful boughs

Lap and listen to a dove's dirge
All her brood smashed by the storm

Lap and listen to a widow wailing
Her man capsized by the battering storm

Lap and listen to elephants trumpeting
Thunder and hail on Vwaza Marsh

Lap, lap you muddy water
Cannot reflect my louring cloud

Lap, lap ripples of Kazuni
Lap against your shaking reeds

The Lingadzi
At Kongwe Mission
(for Jack Chalimba)

(i)

Indeed this river is lovely
So lovely and peaceful.

The water purls tunes
Salutary, and over stones

It leaps sportively like
A hare; then spreads out

Effervescently. Little waves
Ripple out, and out, and out

Then disappear. And slowly
With calm ardour, the water

Traces its windy course
Down to the hungry lake

(ii)

Up the valley and beyond
The wind is a madman

July wind charging at nothing
And craven grass and leaves

Rasp and rattle in terror.
A hill with horns rises high

Piercing the scowling sky.
Under the mellifluous water

Crabs skulk sideways
Around the mossy crags

(iii)

I am listless today,
So cold and listless.

I must rest on this rock,
It's warm on this rock

That never stirs or shifts.
Come Nellie, my poetry,

It's broad and warm
Under the lambent sun.

And what have we
To fear on the rock!

There's nothing to fear
Under the lambent sun

                    Robert Blake, Dowa, 1978

Poetry
(Aretino's Song)

Thou hast married me
To poetry, and to her
Have I poured all my days
A pledge of love

Long sulky days
When I sink
Long bleak nights
When I shrink

My solitude
Draws me deep
Into the warmth
Of the self

Eagle-winged
Soaring high
Above grey clouds

Sweet Jesus
Thou hast married me
To the sublime

To a mellow
Spring singing
Mellifluous songs.

Dear Nellie
(Letter to Nellie when she was in London)

One year seems short
But days are many
Hours so long
And who can count minutes

Outside our house
The wind sighs in trees
Swaying them back and forth
And birds trill

We cultivate around flowers
And daily water them
And slowly they grow
But what homeliness is there

Inside the house
The radio and stereos
Chase away all silence
And meals bring wistful company

Reading and writing
Wake solitude up
My faithful companion
Created before Adam and Eve

I read Seneca and Dostoyevsky
Long into the late hours
When sleep is an illusive lass
And hours a long journey after her

Tired, I toss about in bed
Till Ngcimezi or Dumisa
Sends me on some errand
To the kitchen or fridge

Sleep prefers coming when
Morning peers into windows
And I rise to self-pummelling
Then get ready for work

Since you went away
This has become the song
Of my days and nights
Till you come back

Only our feeble minds
Heighten the sense of gloom
From such needful rehearsals
For longer partings to come

To Mount Coma

Lukonkobe cuts a deep gorge
From the granite heights of Coma
Down the plain to Kasito

Water roars along
Raping the nude slopes
Down to the plain

I paddle my canoe up the river
Against the water and wind
Roaring down to the plain

I paddle through reeds
Bowing and rattling their waists
To the raging water

I paddle up the gorge
To the fountain
Where limpid water springs

There to drink and slake
My thirst, drink
And uplift my soul

Storm

(Ndimwe adada, ndimwe amama
Ndiri mwana winu, adada
Mleke kudinginyika, amama
Ahee! nicali kupenja.)
The lake is rough again:

I set out towards that hill
That olive hill where the sun shines
Brightly over the lush slopes, and
Placid waves caress the sandy shore;
The olive hill where palm fronds
Sigh out a cool breeze; I set out
Paddling my canoe to that hill

But over here winds chasing waters
Like a hound after a doe; swooping
The shore like an eagle after a hen
And waves slapping the shore throwing
Water-arrows leaping like a deer;
Winds chasing waters, toss about
My canoe spattering me with water,
Cold water that drenches me through
And through: my teeth chatter, and
My heart is sore, but I shall not return

I cannot return for I am already lost
I was beckoned away from home; my home
Where the effusion of sunset over Mparayi
Summons everyone to share their meals
And stories; my home where ululations
Of jubilant women welcome hunters,
Our brave hunters as they sing

sidyabeni bobaba
elizwe lechibamu
Mkondo wa m'nakwethu
elizwe lechibamu...

25

I cannot return, I am already lost:
For here are no sandy shores,
But only marshes and mud,
And the croaking toads scoff at
My desolation, the rattling sedge
Sigh no tunes of welcome; I am lost
I cannot return, cannot land, look!
The depressing darkness; how can I land
Where darkness will only squash me
Into the mud! Oh darkness!...Darkness!...

Honeybird

Honeybird you lure me
Away from the morning fire
To the cold wet forest.
On my shoulder, I carry an axe
In my hands, a spear and clubs;
Across the fields to the forest,
Honeybird you lure me on.
Through the forest, up the slopes
The desire for honey, like a fire
In the blood, drives me on.
My knees weak with fatigue, and
A smell of blood in my nostrils,
I look up the high mountain;
Honeybird you lure me on

Zomba CC, 1974

A Goat

I really meant to study.
But a goat, sniffing
All along, came to me;
Then butting me on the back
With its feminine horns
(It almost dashed away
As I swivelled to see it),
Crouched beside me, and
Whimpered all its anxieties
While nibbling at my books.

And I, slow of heart
(Sneezing though, because
Of its overly scented dusts),
But relentlessly consumed
By the fire of sympathy;
How could I study?

Zomba, CC, 1976

Memories of a herdsboy
(for Fulata, Rufu, Kamvwimbi, Kamnkhwara and Mzamani)

(i)

Along these tracks
I walked, whistling
As cattle shuffled
Slowly to pasture

Along these tracks
A boy, wielding a switch
While the sun shone
On beads of dew

Cattle forget
The lightning fury
Of switches landing
On bare backs

Cattle forget,
But the broad back
With hairless lined skin
Tells of hard years

Trees forget
For rains have swept
Dry leaves and twigs
Down the Cabonga

Trees forget,
But for a dent where
I lopped a switch to set
Fire on slow backs

(ii)

To Cimwa valley
Where grass is green
After the first rain
I drove my cattle

Cimwa valley affords
An effusion of green rising
To distant hills that look
Softer than water

There I piped *poliro*
To call fellow herdsboys
Near and far; but no one
Piped back to me

And when clouds
Loured, and birds sang
Of rain, I quickly built
Myself a shack

A small shack
Of branches and palms
Under a deep canopy
Of a *katope* tree

Inside, I stood
Humming tunes to solitude
While stones from heaven
Shredded the leaves

(iii)

Long the hailstorm
And surly flashes cutting
Through the sullen sky
To earth below

Long the hailstorm
The rumbling thunders
And haunting echoes
From dark anthills

How I longed
For a flock of sheep
With a ram to scare
The fire-hawk

Scare him away
Into the forest where
Trees ancient as hills
Parry all blows

Ancient trees
With solid buttresses
And roots that cleave
Through rocks

In pattering rains
The cackling of partridges
And creaking of insects
Warn of sunset

(iv)

Grimly, I discover
That long horns obey
No rain, no lightning
But their bellies

They have gone
And the rain has left
No warm dung, no mark
For me to follow

Pools everywhere
And I run in fast strides;

Perhaps after the anthills
Flies will lead me

But soon darkness
Outlines ghosts lunging
From shrubs; and toads
Bellow weirdly

Suddenly, I hear
My father's anxious call:
Mzondi-o! where are you?
The cattle are home

How ghosts vanish
As I race to him, yet dreading
The stick, for: can those bellies
Skirt all the gardens?

Come Rain

It rained one evening,
Washing away the dust
   from the road
   from trees that line the road;
Washing away rotting leaves,
Washing away cinders
   from hills
   from plains
Washing them down the flooded Lukonkobe;
And Lukonkobe, her waters red,
Patiently carried the dirt
   from Coma and Emteyeni
   down to Engcongolweni
   down to Embombeni
   down to Kasito, Rukuru...
The next day was beautiful:
   the plain and hills cleaned
   the roads and paths cleaned
   the sky and the air cleaned.
Come rain, come
Make the air limpid before me,
Wash my eyes, that I may see.
Flood Lukonkobe
Flood inside me
   these moths and cockroaches
   these lumps of dust in my chest
   these black cinders;
Flood Lukonkobe flood
Clean my inside

The Seed

It has rained so much;
The grass is drooping
Under the weight of raindrops

That mango tree
Burdened with fruit,
Will her young stems
Bear all that fruit?

And my seed,
That seed I planted
Will it germinate?

Reeds of Lukonkobe

Rains come
Flooding Lukonkobe;
Practised reeds bow,
Their leaves shaking with awe
As the mighty waters roar past

Rains go
And reeds that bowed always
Have deformed backs; and
In the dryness of October
They crack and fall
Under their weight

But one day,
From my anthill near Lukonkobe,
As reeds rattled their salute
And nodded to the outraging flood,
I saw one reed
With momentum from four winds
Stand up against the flood

And battered
By the robust waters
The reed was ripped off
And swept down the rivers
Lukonkobe, Kasito, Rukuru
To the lake; where
Sending its roots into the silty shore
It brought forth a new shoot
Dancing gloriously to the breeze

Then I saw
All reeds, like soldiers at attention,
Stand firm against the flood;
As the dammed waters
Spread over the valley

To hide under tall grass,
I heard them whispering
Like toothless hags plotting

Then
From the anthill
Into my bed, I woke
To the awakening day;
To the mooing of cows
As milk-boys cleaned their gourds, ready
To drain every drop from peaceable cows,
But leave intact the udders of those
That fling wild kicks, threatening
To smash cold their male members

And waking to the pen
I wrote:
Rains come
Flooding Lukonkobe...

Why, Oh Why

Daughters of Lukonkobe
Dressed up in colours of flowers
To meet a blind suitor;
Daughters of Lukonkobe
Why, oh why

Mothers of Lukonkobe
Elected an impotent slave
To marry the chief's daughter.
Mothers of Lukonkobe
Why, oh why

Sons of Lukonkobe
Whistled and chanted praises
To embolden a craven bull.
Sons of Lukonkobe
Why, oh why

Men of Lukonkobe
Danced the victorious *mgubo*
To welcome a famished runaway.
Men of Lukonkobe
Why, oh why

Elders of Lukonkobe,
When a he-goat is mad,
Don't you knock off its horns?
Elders of Lukonkobe
Why, oh why

Princes
(Amakhosi balibele nokudhla
Abayazi oluzayo*)

Princes are engrossed
In feasting
They do not notice
Their tower crumbling

Men are engrossed
In wrangling
They do not notice
Spears glaring

Women are engrossed
In gossiping
They do not notice
The baby crying

Boys are engrossed
In frolicking
They do not notice
Their cattle straying

Girls are engrossed
In titivating
They do not notice
Their relish charring

Grey heads are engrossed
In story-telling
They do not notice
Their sun setting

War is Raging

Schools are crafty fingers
That warp our children;
They are a valve against
The outflow of their selves
                    War is raging;
                    Where are you, soldier

Churches overdose us
With bovine patience
As the drover's whip
Drives us to the abattoir
                    War is raging;
                    Where are you, soldier

Roads are Eve's serpents
That lay mirages ahead;
They are a honeybird's song
That transports to poised fangs
                    War is raging;
                    Where are you, soldier

The radio is a hammer
That breaks our spirit;
It is a poisoned arrow
That transmits death to us
                    War is raging;
                    Where are you, soldier

The gods of this land
Fart out darkness;
Their elephant hoofs
Trample the whole land
                    War is raging;
                    Where are you, soldier

Weeds choke our maize
And we cannot clear them;

Birds pick our millet
And we cannot dare cough
                War is raging;
                Where are you, soldier

Our children are drowning
And we cannot rescue them;
They are crying to us
And we can only cry back
                War is raging;
                Where are you, soldier

The law is a watchdog
That always snarls at us
It is a panther that pounces
And locks us in claws
                Guns are rumbling;
                Where are you, soldier

In White

I see them filing out
Like ants from a burning log,
Carrying spades and mattocks.
The scum, in white uniform
Toiling, toiling,
Caged by strong men,
Guns in hands, standing
In dark khaki uniform,
Shod in boots.
It's a hard world,
Brothers; for, who can stand
With impunity against
The harvesting sickle
Of the Law

Across Viyele

My little Marina left at the garage
I now tread footpaths of the people

It is morning of an early October day
And the rains have not yet started

A soft wind combs through gardens
Where black soil is dotted with plants

And the sun is high above Kaning'ina peak
Gazing at the purling Cing'ambo and across

To Viyele valley where sons and daughters
Of the Inkosana pour out a libation of sweat

Many are the sons and daughters of Lubinga
Some hoe bow-bending on knee-high handles

Yet across the Dwangwa our brothers and sisters
Are bundled onto lorries to be tipped in the North

For the beautiful hybrid maize will be choked
If *hinya* weeds are not uprooted from the garden

A youthful woman with a pert smile marks me
As I saunter along her maize and beans garden

She spins a lively greeting across my path
And startled I answer with a distant look

She is certain she used to see me in Zomba
And before she curses my memory I move on

I know women who would pounce on a man
Whose love has gone years and oceans away

An old woman on the next portion of maize
Works as if this was a means of penance

And I remember Ago-Mbizi my mother-in-law
I remember Ago-Phakati all alone at home

Slowly pinching her skin together all over
And slowly sucking in her cheeks and lips

How do you care for a widowed mother
To keep loneliness from eating her up

To stop her scratching the sun-baked soil
With a tool handed down from ancestors

After the gardens a boy in school uniform
Looking after a bull and two or three cows

Chants a reggae tune with Ngoni fire
And cows moo in unison: *bo-rn to su-ffer*

A boy conducting a choir away from school
Saturates the morning air with bitter cud

On the road a Benz zooms into the new city
So indifferent are backs sinking into luxury

Mzuzu TTC, 1989

Hegel and Marx

(A picture from the
 Educational Times)

Hegel
Is tall
And rare
Like a deep
Sky. In all
He levitates
Towards
The sky.

Marx
Is short
And burly
Like a dense
Sky. In all
He gravitates
Towards the
Ground.

Leeds University, 1981

Martyrs
Pakupoka Wanangwa
Pali suzgo na viphyo
(For the Rev. Dr. S. Chiphangwi, on his Martyrs' Day sermon, 1981; service attended by Dr.Kamuzu Banda)

Songs on the radio
Raise our hearts high
To the praise of martyrs

The word of the preacher
Reminds us of our debt
To those who died for freedom

Martyrs are everywhere
In Uganda, Zimbabwe, South Africa
Chiradzulu, Ntcheu, Nkhata Bay...

But are they also martyrs
Who died for an unknown cause
That shall never be realised

                    *   *   *

Chilembwe fumes at *Thangata*
Chilembwe pounces on Listonya
Chilembwe slays Listonya

A furious mob rushes at the Dona
The mob knock down the Dona
And cut *mphini* on the white thighs

Chilembwe rescues the Dona
Chilembwe sets her on a horse
The horse gallops to Limbe

Gallops straight into the train
Gallops to Salisbury, Cape Town
Gallops home to Great Britain

Guns rumble over Chiradzulu
But Chilembwe is inside the bell
And later gallops to America

*   *   *

Mumba organised the NAC
Mumba phoned the white Queen
Mumba was invited to London

And the natives threw a tea-party
To bid him successful voyage
But they put poison in his tea

At Cidikalala women and men
Gathered to see the Madang'ombe
And bid him *paweme* to London

Children danced round the van
Puffing slowly into the village, but
They did not see the Madang'ombe

And when the van was opened
They saw a shiny boat-like box
To ferry him on the voyage across

*   *   *

Chilembwe is coming again
In the flashing of lightning
Furious against *Thangata*

These belching estate owners
With fleets of lorries and trailers
Ferrying tobacco to the auction

Batten on unshod tenants
With shorts dangling precariously
From their scrawny waists

When Chilembwe comes again
And Levi Mumba of Lukonkobe
What song shall we sing to them

                    *   *   *

Our villages that reared martyrs
Have become ruins where mice
Squeak at the idea of martyrdom

And sons and daughters of the craven
Have snatched the hunter's portion
Listen to their deafening song and drum

True, we are tough-skinned people
Baked in the kiln of hardships
And our backs are trained in stooping

But how long shall a hunting-dog
Relish chewing a clean bone
When cockroaches fatten on meat

Elegy to Fanikiso
Part I: Hunger, stones and bullets

How long must the dialogue between
Stones and bullets be conducted before
Our authorities awaken to the danger

How long will our children be raised
On the market culture but be killed
For buying what we do not approve

How many millions must be squandered
On reviving a reign of terror while women
With faint babies stampede for maize bran

Amidst the touted donor aid police reforms
How long will the police loot democracy
By killing the weak to protect the powerful

How many task forces before we understand
That planting seeds of hate only increases
Our harvest of hunger poverty and death

How long how long this chasing of escaping
Rats and cockroaches while a conflagration
Is blowing our nation into smoke and ashes

Is it regionalism when one cries, fire, fire
And sprints for the hosepipe to direct
A jet into the fiery bowels of the dragon

Is this politics: this belching and farting
This looking around in a scowl, spitting
Then blaming opposition for the stench

Oh our megalomaniac old man, you left us
And these yellow-bellied leaders, how long
Will it take them to rise above their pockets

Part II: Jackals, mandazi and helicopters

We shudder when the hen withdraws
Her wings and beckons cruel claws
To swoop and seize struggling chicks

When the jackal agitates black ants
Poking his long tail into their nest
To extract mouthfuls and chew them

When mothers in khakis of seniority
Rape democracy by ordering teargas
On the starveling crying out for food

When our savants towering over corridors
Of erudition fine-hone youthful brains
And then deliver them to the butcher

Isn't our police a foreign invading force
Have they ever had a child or relation
In the university to see innocent tears

Yet before sunrise their wives and kids:
Writhing disfigured bundles of poverty
Heave logs of pine from Zomba Mountain

Their verandas a smoke screen of cheap
Sizzling oil burning *mandazi* for sale
By truant pupils at the stage and taverns

How long will the police defend the criminal
Poverty while Mercedes, Vx's and copters
Dry coffers with endless political campaigns

Or is it the eruption of long bottled bitterness:
This savagery misdirected to the innocent
Like a chained dog that attacks its liberator

xxxx

Part III: Umhlaba kaunoni

Fanikiso, your name tells of a semblance
Of death as the earth's insatiable belly
Swallows up bodies but never grows fat

After a long wait of years and semesters
Your parents were now ready to embrace
The graduate son in their thatch house

But you bent to lift a schoolboy in blood
With a bullet in his neck, not fearing
That another was aimed at your heart

Fanikiso, their bullets have hawk's eyes
And talons that snatch us from high
When hidden even amongst a thousand

Your peers battled with a legion of fiends
They bulldozed boulders onto the roads
Boulders Napolo tossed from the mountain

But they were armed to the beak, the vultures
Blasting teargas into lecture-rooms and hostels
Their black Marias zooming over the boulders

Fanikiso, the Friday you died the rain came
And even the hungry found maize to plant
If only to preserve a little seed for next year

Monday, and the police invaded again, ordering
The colleges closed within two hours, offering
Teargas and bullets to those from far, stranded

Clement Matemvu was forced to ride the monster
That slaughters but never eats: monster of the road
Killed finalist Matemvu - another teacher wasted

xxxx

Part IV: Yesu wane wandicema, nkuruta...

My Jesus has called me, I'm going to my Saviour...
A choir of students sang around the white coffin
On a table draped in a blue silver jubilee cloth

Bus loads of students from the constituent colleges
Taking the remains across police road blocks
To the North affirmed the true spirit of Malawi

And they say (the man said) he is so disturbed
Because students looted a shop of beers, but
For the murder he sent not even a sympathy

The radio aired earsplitting lies of a spokesman
Alleging rape amidst a storm of stones and bullets
And blaming the marksmen for shooting only two

And a commission was appointed to fulminate
Against students for lighting a torch in darkness
And the staff who helped to calm the students

Yet even during the days of the Lion students
Demonstrated at the college and central office
And stormed the town with songs of liberation

Across the Likangala to the cathedral they danced
The celebration of the Bishops' era-marking letter
But the police controlled with no bullets or teargas

Fanikiso, the *Sikusinja* bird sings in the tree
Your blood is a seed planted, like the blood
Of Soweto children singing in a hail of bullets

Your name, like Chilembwe, Mumba, Chipembere,
Chisiza, Ching'oli, Mhango, Matenje ...Matafale
Is our anthem of light in this cave we call Malawi.

Zomba, CC 2002

51

The Face of Epiphania

Part I: *Lirani aMalawi, lirani...*

The face of girl in angelic white with a rosary
Stares the nation from the front page of a daily

The blood of a girl, innocent and beautiful
Is a cross of red that marks our democracy

Ten-year old, she did not vote against anyone
She did not demonstrate against the winners

Happy child, playing ball around the house
Why did the bullet snatch her youthful life

Orphan girl, sinking in a shroud of our hatred
Black smoke coiling to swallow the rising sun

Now, who will console her aunt, her cousins
Their hearts bleeding, and their heads reeling

Is this our beloved Malawi: a monster nation
That devours its own people, its own children

Yet for months, people prayed for the election
People fasted: but where did all the prayers go

****

Part II: *a-Morotoni, nyanga babika m'nkhokwe...*

How easy it is to point a finger to the warlock
While three are bent back towards the pointer

How easy to point a finger to brazen rogues
Who sell our heirlooms to monsoon pedlars

Point a finger at the old serpent we thought
Decapitated, still rearing its tribalistic head
And the guest who leaves a stench at farewell
Outdoing what pervaded his entire visitation

Oh good people, after bashing the great lion
Is this season for bashing Munganya-muweme

While mice were squeaking in the granary, mating
Was that not the time to introduce the whiskers

Now, lawsuits every day: even those who bought
Favours have become Jehus driving the man hard

Oh foolish worshippers: how did you think a goat
Could keep vigil over your malted millet flour

****

Part III: *Za-sin-tha! U-def, Boma!*

True, we have an oversupply of chameleons
Who transmogrify when their pockets yawn

Have scoundrels shaking hands under the table
And sealing obscene marriages with hollow hugs

Slimy amphibians, minions of the old crocodile
Trying to rebuild a monolith the people pulverised

A kitchen cabinet teaming with fat cockroaches
You flush out many, but more crawl in at night

A reformed police slow to apprehend criminals
But always quick to teargas and kill the innocent

An army good at keeping peace in foreign lands
While at home a brute force preys on the citizens

53

But the blood of Epiphania, the blood of Fanikiso
Of Matafale and many will stir us for the march

For look: the man we did not blow the horn for
Wields the spear, marching steadfast to the drum

Zomba CC, 2004

What shall we say

When falsehood was true
We chuckled day and night
We chuckled and whispered
For what did we know

When darkness was light
We fumbled day and night
We fumbled and stumbled
For what did we see

When sadness was joyful
We simpered day and night
We simpered and sniffled
For what did we feel

When bitterness was honey
We choked day and night
We choked and coughed
For what did we taste

Now that truth has become lies
We mumble day and night
We mumble and stutter
For what shall we say

Eyes of Age

Youth waxed us with ideals
But age has shown us the real

Love is a maiden's song
Of an eagle beyond the clouds

Beauty is a boy's dream
Of a dove beyond mountains

Generosity burns to stumps
Fingers trying to stretch out

Charity is the arrogance driving
Those who keep others indebted

Unity is a shadowy pool where
Minorities are silently drowned

Truth is what lions posit
And that which guns guard

Lies are the bulwark of power
Crowned with a veneer of gold

Equanimity is the diamond tip
Tapering arrows of suffering

It draws out poetry from anger
Coiling out of incinerated hopes

The Self

Consolidation of the self
Is a great moral effort.

Society is a monstrosity
Demanding propitiation

From individuals. Society
Is a faceless progression

Annihilating individuals.
The individual, rarefied

Of all corruption, is the self.
And solitude is the culture

For the sublimation of the self.
The self is his own identity

And poetry is his own bride,
His song of a velvet sunrise.

Love is a mellifluous
River that purifies all;

It is a titillation of light
That sweetens solitude.

It rejuvenates the self
To flow into poetry.

Freedom is the government
Of the self. And equanimity

Is the power of rectitude;
It is the self's own fortitude.

Old Age

Is it ashen hair, crackling backs, and haunting
Echoes of hopes shrivelled in the hot sun

A net cast wide across the vast water
Surges and bulges as it slowly pulls along

Then it pours out water on the dry sand
Before folding up into a clumsy heap. No

Old age is a catch of water hyacinth, skulking crabs
And few fish writhing amongst vomiting condoms

                                        Zomba, CC, 2003

Nothing

How I wish
I delved into the crater
Of the rainbow
To reach for eggs
Of the lightning!

Oh ambition,
Daughter of tantalising heights:
You wax me with zealous wings
To fly high
When the sun is blazing!

Oh hope,
Glittering dew
Promising diamonds,
You split and melt
Into nothing

Zomba, CC, 1977

Light and Darkness

Light is air rarefied
Light, and the residue

Darkness - black mote
In the wind blowing

Blowing to darken
The sky. Dear Lord

My soul in this sod
My soul condensed

In this tall clay, flows
To Thy light; rarefy it

Into fire, blue flame
In lilac frame, burning

Always burning, never
Obsequious to hollow clay.

Rarefy it, for this marriage
With the sod - the two

Can never become one -
Has born many a tear.

My Soul

A glade, sheen-lit
In a deep forest:

Solarium of solace.
Bent, languid I come

Like a moth to light.
Here's my face, old

And dry like a cicada's;
My heart is in this sack.

Here's my hollow soul
In a tattered paper bag.

I've failed to strike unity
For fear of inhibition.

Branches ramify from
Trunks, and leaves

In shrilling winds
Militate against twigs.

True unity is elusive
Like a sweet dream.

From the glade, voice
Of Light: my dear son

Grass is always scrubby
Where trees are dense.

Lightning is a tomahawk
Always whacking to splinters

The splendour of trees
Towering over grasslands.

So grass to grass, trees
To trees, and let leaves

Be leaves, twigs be twigs;
But all grow towards light

My Star

White clouds
Cover dark mountains
Of hate; it's a shame

I sat in smoke
Black soot
All over my body

Darkened; my skin
Smells of soot:
Who can look at me

In darkness?
Who can talk to me
In darkness?

Lorn shall I stand
In the rain, in
White skeins from high

Ablution for sin.
A star shall be born
To me; shining star

Who can hold it back?
Mountains of envy
Cannot shade the light

My bright star
Will shine a halo
Around my head

Songs of Seasons

(i)

In the beginning is the ending
In the ending is the beginning
For the wheel of time rolls on
And on, rolling always forwards
Which is indeed backwards, for
The circumference is the same
Described by the locus of time.
Men hold fast to the cogs of time,
Tumbling men counting their days,
Which are sulky days of loneliness
And bleak days of tears, counting
Their days and waiting for the best
To come from the worst; men high
And low, all tantalised by felicity!
Men of this earth cannot see mountains
And valleys of their days converging
To a stubborn question-mark

(ii)

Christmas comes, and then New Year,
New Year comes, and then Christmas
For the wheel of time has no head
No tail, for the distance is the same
Covered over and over; yet the question
Shall still come: the Son is coming
To you, have you prepared the room?
Prepare it now, for the sun shall set
And behind the delectable moonlight
Is cold gloom, where stars are nebulous;
The sun shall set over the cold sea
And the moon shall lay ghastly figures
On the water-mirror. Prepare the room,

Hezekiah on his death-bed listened
To Isaiah, and prepared his room;
Hence the sun of his life went back

The ending of year is the beginning
Of another, the ending of day ,which
Is the beginning of night, the question
Is a slippery path for the night-walker
When owls hoot; brother, sister
Have you prepared your room?
Look, Christmas is here, but the son
Wanders in the cold, in the rain
Knocking at door after door, in the dark
The son wanders from house to house;
Shunned by all, yet all celebrate His Coming
Shrugged by all who celebrate His Coming:
Those who flood post offices with cards
Of good wishes; those who multi-colour
Their rooms with cards; the party-lovers
And those who seek oblivion, drowning
Their selves in bottles of madness;
Those who spend prurient nights in dark
Rooms of our come-all sisterhoods,
And those who sing sweet carols
In drowsy churches; all celebrate
His coming, and all shall answer

(iii)

At the beginning of the year
Which is the ending of another
Resolutions are always made
Noble resolutions which but soon
Are trampled down by hectic days;
And the wheel rolls on and on
Tossing ambitious of callow minds
To frustrations, but still we hold on
To the cogs swishing us around
To the ending which is the beginning

Indeed this year has gone
The harsh year of big tears
Has gone; oh, how many have
Fallen in it! Enigmatic men
Wielding Gelasian swords, men
With charisma who led their people
Through dark days; this year
Has indeed gone; welcome New Year,
We see your streaks penetrating,
Streaks of peace as the Nile
Washes away blood, the blood
Of many, shed for the spread
Of hate; we see streaks of peace
As the Zambezi washes away the blood
Of brothers to the Indian Ocean

Bless them all; bless all of them
Who wave white, who hold high white
Feathers to lands torn apart by strife
As brothers stalk brothers, lands drowned
In the blood of many sacrificed on the altar
Of hate; bless them. And do not forget
Those from across oceans our fathers welcomed
Long long ago, allowing them hectares and
Hectares of our rich velds; remember them
For now they stand astride our gold mines
Our diamond mines, and bundle us, our helpless
Women, old men and crying children to hustle
Us into dry patches where dongas yawn out diseases
And famine. Do not forget those that clothe the naked
And feed the famished with promises and chains.
And remember our friends from across oceans
Who aid us with automatics to track each other
Like antelopes of the wild our forefathers tracked
With simple spears and arrows; remember them Lord

(iv)

In the ending of year is the beginning
Of another, the beginning of a new year
When heavy rain pours down sweeping clean
The slopes and plains, and washing away
Dry leaves, ash, and cinders of wild fires;
And dust from tracks dug deep by hoofs
Of cattle and goats that scuttle away from
Whips wielded with abandon, whips that
Sting like a swarm of hornets on backs
And sides shorn bare; sweeping clean
Paths dug deep by feet of women who uphold
Life of the village, as open lilac fires crackle
Firewood on verandas; paths dug deep by the feet
Of girls gracefully balancing pots of water
Up the steep slopes from Lukonkobe

In the beginning of year when rain pours
Down incessantly, Lukonkobe is the broad
Back on which paths, brooks and streams
Hustle their dirt, the back that bears all
To the sandy Kasito, as rain pours down
And dissolves dust to leave the air limpid

(v)

At the ending of rains is the coming
Of Easter when the question probes deep
And deep into sore hearts: the Tree abounds
With Grace, have you prepared your room?
Prepare it now, this is the right time for you:
Look at the Tree, look to the right,
Salvation is there; why do you despair?
Do not shed tears, salvation is there.
Look at the Tree, look to the left,
Damnation is there; why do you presume?
Do not smile smugly, damnation is there

The ending of rains when brightly coloured
Birds sing perching on grass laden with dew;
Grass, forming domes above paths every morning
To chill a passer-by with baptism. The ending
Of day is the beginning of night, and the question
Is a paved way for those who prepared the room
For the Risen Saviour; and they shall sing:

Ciuta ndi linga lithu, Movwiri mu suzgo
Nanga caru cisezgeke, ise nta titope

They shall sing, to the ending of night
Which is the beginning of day; they shall sing.

Salima S S, 1978

New Year
(for Nellie)

Outside my house
Children in dirty clothes
Hailing the new year
Dance in the mud

From house to house
An old man in rags
His pockets flapping
Dances like a skeleton

Dances invoking pity
Like funeral dances:
Rattling scarecrow, not here;
Take this coin, and go!

At midnight
Shouts, gongs and bells
And amidst the din
A gun exploded

Welcome New Year
How much rain do you bring?
Will the water settle my heart
Torn between joy and fear?

I have prayed and wept
Entering the New Year;
Christ in the garden, prayed
And prayed, sweating blood

I have prayed and wept
Entering this year: the fear
Of bleeding to stone-dryness,
When one has loved so much

Salima Sec School, 1978

Christmas

Your Excellency, Doctor Bee
Landing majestically on my jam
And sucking out the sweet juice
While poising your sting
To terrorise me

Tell me
Do women not sing
And dance to ecstasy
In praise of your craft
At making honey

Do they know that
You steal the sweet juice
While dropping bitter pollens
From your soiled body
To sour my jam

Now look
Two others swoop down
Buzzing furiously at me
Before landing on my jam
With stings poised

Yet the hotel
Has cards with ribbons
And lights of all colours
Draped on pine branches
Proclaiming peace

And the radio
Sings about a manger
Where a king was born
To give to the world
Love and freedom

Oh my Lord
I cannot move my hand

Cannot even utter a word
For fear of agitating the air
Around poised stings

How can I
Be free and love
In this land where freedom
Love and peace are clouds
Bringing no rain

Lilongwe Hotel, December 1991

The Road to Emmaus
(for Easter: Luke 24:13-35)

On this winding road
A shadow is close by me

On this lonesome road
A shadow trails after me

Extending from my heels
East to the sun's cradle

And now the sun is setting
Slowly into lurid clouds

Spread behind the ridge
That sends out darkness

A shadow is close by me
On this wandering road

Yet darkness attracts me
As flames attract a moth

Oh my Lord, draw nigh
On this road to Emmaus

The Voice

Again the voice said
Write a new song
For my people to sing

Write for those who wake
Before birds have sung
To scratch and plant

For those whose backs
Must soak and steam
From sunrise to sunset

For those who must spit
Into cracked palms
Until their mouths dry

For those who dress
Like scarecrows but
Gather much for others

And write for those
Who sow only a handful
But gather in lorryfuls

For those whose crop
Is watered and nourished
By the sweat of others

For those who conjure up
Ecstasies of loyalty
By dropping a sweet

And write a chorus
For those who chastise
With hornets and scorpions

Teach Them

And a voice said
Teach them about fire,
Take them to the hot point
Where right crosses wrong
And the result is fire

Teach them
Not to swallow whole
These striplings fixed
On wooden forms,
Moronic

Teach them
1 + 1 kindle flames
Burning to zero.
Command them

To burn all books
Cheating about mathematics:
For what is addition
And multiplication
To poor people?
Things are always
Snatched from them.

What is subtraction
And division
To the rich?
They clutch at
All good things.

Tell them
Mathematics
Is the art of buffoons.
Train them

To develop X-ray eyes
That see maggots wiggling

Inside Grey Heads

Train them to see
The double-tongued
Snake hissing in the grass;
See man double-tongued:
Spinning one on smiling lips
And coiling another in the heart.

Teach them Caesarean
These vamps with
Men-pregnancies of years
Overdue, bulging
In bat-flaps, tied.

Caution them,
Those tethers have snapped
And words are at large again

Words:
Voluble canines
Breaking bones;
Voluble poultices
Soothing and healing flesh
Over broken bones.
Caution them

Never to look
To the sky
For lightning
Signs us off
On dark tablets of clouds
And thunderbolts
Shake the very roots
Of hope.

Train to Balaka

A train puffs round
And up the slopes

Its stubborn will, steel
Wheels that carry it along

So many wheels squeak
Under its millipede body!

                ******

A boy sits, sucking mango
After mango, while belching

And green flies swarm
The coach: so noisome!

                ******

A young woman scrambles in
Her beauty drowned in poverty

Only a worn out wrapper
From breasts to above knees.

In her hands, a smiling baby
Nude and round as a pumpkin:

A fruit thriving in the wild,
Lord, where is the sower

The roving sower who never
Deigns to come back and tend.

                ******

To love someone
What a commitment!

Christ on the Rood
Have patience with us

For days are so many
Fewer the hairs of a bull.

Some day we shall know;
Then love shall drive us

And love shall steer us
Like wheels of a train

Hen's Dropping

Boyi
drudges for them
day and night

wakes at five
and retires
well after dark

during the night
must make rounds
when dogs bark

never grumbles
except on
pay overdue

yesterday
after the pay
ran like mad

in Limbe
shop after shop
was baffled

must slave away
for yet another month
to buy a shirt

man emasculated
of all power before
enticing windows

walks home
in fanning scarecrow
shirt and trousers

who is there
needs no moment
to feel grand

in drunken houses
all are welcome
to forget their woes

worries dissolve
in dehydrating waters
but all the money

evaporates
only to condense
more woes tomorrow

at midnight
was swept away
like droppings

the cold wind
of long dark hours
blew in reality

Blantyre TTC 1983

A Widow

An old widow walking to the market.
She must keep on her head a heavy basket
To keep her children in school.
I saw her down the road
Going to sell her maize.

Her face
        where many sorrows brood
Is cracked and scratched
        with claws of the cruel cold;
Her hands
        the dirty and coarse hands
        for those whose are clean
Have grown thick and callous;
The soles of her feet
        without hope for shoes
Have grown thick tissues.
An old widow tramping
        her neck deep into shoulders
Down the road to the market.

But suddenly an eardrum rending hoot,
Helter-skelter to surrender their road
        but near the edge she stumbles;
Then in a slouch she stands
        enjoying the heat radiating
        from her nail-off bleeding toe;
Her maize scattered on the dust.
Then a Benz zooms past;
On the backseat, a mastiff:
        the type that eat money a week
        enough to keep her children in school.

Submerged in the dust, she slits her eyes;
Then suddenly opens them

to a big bang sound!
Hobbles to see, though
                what ill can befall them?
Then walking some yards, she sees
                the triumph over terrain
                the luxury of travelling
Crushed against a huge trunk.
All around
                smashed glass scattered;
Inside squashed steel
                man and dog locked
                in a bloody hug.

Song of Orphan Boy
(Ng'ombe, apa mukulira ng'ombe, nkayitorenku?)

A cow
Now that you
Demand a cow;
Where shall I
Get it from

A cow
When my father
Departed already;
Where shall I
Get it from

A cow
You stick to it
Like a tick;
Where shall I
Get it from

A cow
Lice-crusher me
The fireside my bed;
Where shall I
Get it from

A cow
When nieces of wives
Warm husbands with kraals;
Where shall I
Get it from

A cow
And I pluck a zither
All night long;
Where shall I
Get it from

A cow
When my love song
Wells out from my eyes;
Where shall I
Get it from

A cow
When a few grey hairs
Tell of wasted seasons;
Where shall I
Get it from

A Modern Lullaby
(Wamwana leka kulira...)

Lool lool lool
Good baby, stop crying
Your mother is gone to school
To school across land and waters
Across waters in a heavy bird, flying

Happy baby, stop crying
Your mother is coming soon
Coming with fast toys flashing
And cards singing fourth birthday
And will give you a huge hug, crying

Baby, why do you cry
Your loving father is here
Here to sing you a new lullaby
Lullaby to wipe your tears and his
His tears until the heart grows dry

Baby, will you not cheer up
Your father cannot cuddle you
To his hairy chest giving not a sup
For the ancient design forgot breasts
Now baby, when will you shut up

My Man
(Omunaanga nchiyani)

What is this
My man, what is this
What is this now
The shirt is tight

To the other wife
You went yesterday
And you return today
The stomach swollen

What is it
My man, what is it
What is it now
The shirt is tight

Tale of Nyavitima

Once upon a time
There was love, and love
Whispered only sweetness

The sun rose bright
And cool rivers mirrored
White clouds sailing high

Love is like a tree growing
Which soon bears flowers
Pouring out aroma of beauty

Winds sigh in the trees
And birds trill in the branches
As day passes and night comes

In the night there are moths
That plant ravenous grubs
To gnaw away at the roots

Children, if you see love wilting
Do not ask questions; only
Remember once upon a time

Nyumbani's Tale
(In Memory of Dada H. Nyumbani Shatira)

Trappist went to the river
In the heat of early afternoon

There he came near a burrow
With footprints of monitor lizard

He examined these footprints
Showing monitor was in the burrow

Then he said as if to himself
Yet shouting for monitor to hear

I will bring and set my trap
Before monitor crawls out today

Meanwhile he quickly set the trap
And tip-toed to under a shade

Monitor had overheard the plan
And reasoned from inside the hole

I must run out of this grave
Before he brings his death tools

He crawled out of darkness
Hoping he was going into light

The trap was keen for his neck
It snapped and throttled him

Dangling he gasped for breath
His eyes and forked tongue out

From his shade under a *katope* tree
Trappist dashed towards his catch

How quickly I have got him today
See his double tongue flickering

I have got the skin to make a drum
That will call everyone to dance

Panted out monitor in a dying voice
It's you who have the double tongue

From your lips shine out hope
From your heart creeps out death

Little Frog
(Kacule ka mdambo)

Little frog of the river
Saw cattle grazing patiently
  Low dewlaps dangling up the valley

Little frog of the river
Wondered why he did not have
  Long horns pointing up the valley

Little frog of the river
Splashed some water, to stir
  Long tails whisking up the valley

Little frog of the river
Started bellowing, to agitate
  Calm humps undulating up the valley

Little frog of the river
Puffed up his belly, to frighten
  Blank eyes blinking up the valley

Little frog of the river
Burst like a puffed-up balloon
  Unheard by ears flapping up the valley

Ago-Cimara's Tale

(In memory of
Gogo Rabeka Cimara Khomboka NyaKumwenda)

A man and Kaluphya became friends,
Close friends, my children:
Place your foot where I place mine

Kaluphya invited the man to his home,
His fiery home, my children:
Roast a cock and roast a he-goat

Kaluphya welcomed his friend with dances,
Come-and-see dances, my children:
The moon adds agility and style to dancers

Then the man invited Kaluphya home,
His tinder home, my children:
Plate of okra must go in order to come

Dancers were called to welcome the guest,
Welcome Kaluphya, my children:
The elegance of steps is in boxes from Jubeki

The man entertained Kaluphya to a feast,
A sumptuous feast, my children:
Come parched throats and salivating mouths

Kaluphya must sit on bare ground,
In open space, my children:
To wrap him tight who bursts enclosures

A big kraal was surrounded by huts,
A huddle of huts, my children:
With walls of poles and roofs of grass

Inside the kraal Kaluphya sat on a stool,
A wooden stool, my children:
As dancers raised dust from dry dung

Wiggling waists fanned his eyes,
His fiery eyes, my children:
Devoured their dangling wrappers

Soon the whole kraal was on fire,
A fierce fire, my children:
Tongues rumbled over the huts

And the tale of friendship with Kaluphya;
With wildfire, my children,
Ends in tears and had-I-known ashes

Daughter of Sunshine
(for Nellie)

Like a chivalrous knight
Rescuing a lass from a dragon
Have I fought this battle,
My double-edged sword
Striking from depth of seas
To heights of heaven

Long a nymph lay
Confined in a deep cavern
Up the brow of Mparayi
Singing in darkness

And a voice said to me:
Go up the precipice
For thou must deliver her
From the hands of centaurs
In the dark cavern,
Deliver her.

And like Jonah
I shuddered to imagine
How I could scale
The slippery precipice:
Oh, what bravado!

And those fierce centaurs
Kindling fire with their hoofs
As they charged out of caves
Their bows tautly drawn!
Could I fight them?

From Lukonkobe
Mermaids dancing
To hot tunes of Eros
Whispered to me: come...

But that voice again
Go!

O, beauty
Not marred by darkness
But perfected:
Look!. . . .

She saved me from wandering;
Like poet Aengus, wandering

I was a lonely god
Visiting shrine after shrine
Seeking fellowship. But adorers
Blind to divine presence
Threw cold ash at me

She has saved me;
My queen, my sheen
Crowning the peak
Of emerald beauty;
Daughter of sunshine,

My heart has found peace
Since I shook hands with you

Bells

Bells are tolling
Gentle bells calling
The wanderers, the strayed
Following winds blowing
From without, dogging
Into the maze of forest
Where rasping leaves
Irritate the ears;
The maze of forest where
Shrilly songs of cicadas
Grate all hope of water

Bells are calling
Guiding bells we hear
With our eyes full of light;
Yet, how we stumble
Like a bat in bright light
Bumping from wall to wall
And then crashing down
Near a window wide open
To let it out into streets
Lined with neon lights
Where swarm flying ants
Pairing to nuptial bliss.

The Desert
(for Nellie)

Long I lay
In Sahara wilderness
And freezing nights
And burning days
Seared me to a cyst

I lay shrivelled
Under thwarting dunes,
And shrilling winds
Scooping the sand
Dug me up, only
To bury me deep

I lay insensible
Under frigid sand
Under torrid sand
As sandstorms tore
Across the vastness

In the dry vastness
Glances of mirages
Provide uplifts,
And stars at night
Give sense of direction
To a desolate Hagar

I was a reject
Lost in the wilderness
Tossed about by storms
Trodden under hoofs,
As I lay in oblivion
Devoid of hope

She touched me, touched
Me with a rejuvenating
Touch, and sunset over

The olive hills anointed me
With yellow oil, to soften
And remove my cyst

Goddess of oases
Of deep fountains
Nurturing the vast
Dryness; my nymph
You have revived me
With your touch
Softer than oil.

She has Come
(for Yananda)

She was born in September
The sylph of Lukonkobe.

St. John's, Mzuzu: ethereal,
Cool, a garland of greenery

In a chamber my sheen lay
Attended by nurses and a doctor

With a vacuum pump. I stood outside
The door; shouldn't enter: STAFF ONLY

Son of the Virgin in the stall,
Extend delivering hands over her,

And your calm over us of Lukonkobe
Our anxious hearts having ascended

To the mouth, where words
Freeze on the lips. Ears are sharp

Even to the sigh of silence
From the chamber. A smiling

Nurse popping out titillates
Our taut nerves. She has come:

Anxious hearts descend home
At last; she has finally come,

Oh mystery! She has borne me
To the honour of fatherhood,

And father's mother, long gone,
Has returned today; Yananda,

Mother of Luhlaba, the earth,
Is back: Glory be to His Name!

Engcongolweni Village, 1978

In Praise of Linley Mbano
(by a man from Kasungu)

This girl only
This girl only at humility
At humility as such
She drank it all

Somewhere else
A secondary school girl
Would never greet any
Man or woman

But this girl only
This girl only at discipline
At discipline as such
I take off my hat

Thank you

**(for gifts received on our
25th marriage anniversary)**

Dear friends and relatives
The real value of your gifts
Goes far beyond the material
For they illuminate your prayers
And emblazon love on our hearts

As we sing our silver season
Delving in the depth of His love
A sheen of sunlight pours out
To touch our friendship afresh

Yours Nellie and Zondiwe

Wedding in Town

So we attended their wedding
Nellie and I remained calm amid
Exhilarating colours and songs

The queen in immaculate white
Dazzled my stoic king, smiling
Magnanimously in his black suit

The room went wild with ululations
As slow, slow, they walked along
Attended by singing seraphim

King and queen reigning supreme
In a world of smiles, colours
And roses nurtured in camaraderie

And to sit down was a ceremony
Demanding wads of notes
To be surrendered to the table

******

Time for *pelekani* ; and we rose
Walking off beat to the song
As we went with our humble gifts

At home, when we were young
Songs of *majure,* the beat
Of *ndelerita,* drove us to ecstasy

******

Flashes of cameras held time still
As they stood, hand over hand
For the mystic ceremony of the cake

Then we drank to their happiness
While spirits of the Anglo-Saxons
Sizzled their blessings from bottles

At the end of it all, what remains:
Heaps of money for paying debts
And a future that spurns all pomp

Salima SS, 1978

Dust of Terrain

There are days
We swim in joy, days
We levitate in bliss
With light hearts

There are days
We fill depressions
With streams of tears
And sink so deep

Leviathan has wings
Waxed on his sides
Soars above mountains

Soars towards stars
And knows no tears
To sink his hollow heart,

Stars stare the sea:
An insatiable monster
Always sucking rivers
Valleys and plains dry

Under the dark sky
The scorpion constellation
Raises his virulent sting
Ready to jet out fire

Dust of terrain
Shall never
Challenge stars
Nor ever settle there

Decay

A deep forest:
Long have I stood here
Lost in thought.

Ramifications spread
Umbrellas of green
Above which flowers

Smile to sunshine;
Umbrellas casting
A deep shadow,

A shadow of gloom.
I have stood here
My body feeling dark;

Have stood where
Gloom shrouds odours
From a process

Ancient as life
Where flies, and lizards
Link the chain

To a baboon
Bowed to Decay,
Who unmake us.

Vipya
(Ooo Vipya, Vipya wabazungu)

Ooo Vipya
Vipya of the whiteman
Conqueror of the lake

Welcomed *machona*
From the bowels of gold
To bury them in the lake

Ooo Vipya
Heavy roaring iron
Ironing the waves

Vipya of the whiteman
Mass iron coffin
Deep under the lake

Tears in the Wilderness
(for Deborah and Masida)

Wretched she stands
In a forest of strangers, wailing
In a strange tongue.

Love had called; she followed
But now, so early, her cord
With them has snapped

And a red mound
Has put them asunder:
Tears do not bind.

Fanny in the wilderness
Call loud, and loud
Do not fear: Jesus is there

xxx

In town, there are friends
And honeybird friends
At weekends, who lure you

To ride the darkness.
A horse galloped along
The streets of Limbe

A horse, white and wild
Dashed him cold
Near the Cathedral.

Oh, this sad yoke
A thirst has laid
On the necks of men!

At his home, fingers
Pointed at witchcraft
Lying at a corner.

Salima SS, March 1978

106

My Father
(Mateyo Mbano)

(i)

The coldness of death gives courage
Much more than the warmth of life

Your face glimmered with calm
And you tried to smile as I came in

You assured me you were all right
Except that your feet felt cold

The next day I bought a blanket
Thinking it was the coldness of July

Father, here is a blanket for you
It will shield your feet from July

But you gave me an ironical smile
And stared beyond the warmth of blankets

(ii)

Luhlaba, Chione, Mateyo, my father
Do you hear when I call you by name

Where are those vivid reminiscences
Of a boy whose uncles cast into a pool

Of a keen scholar returned from Khondowe
Because his guardian drowned in a calabash

An overseer of estates in Mozambique
Riding in a trolley pushed by men

A senior postmaster special first class
Over some whites during colonial era

How we enjoyed your reminiscences
Told with the freshness of a new song

(iii)

Early on the 5th of August, 1988
Men from home outside my house

Men knocking and whispering together
On a cold morning of a shrouded Friday

Their faces give out the whole message
Before the mouth adds in the details

In the dead of night he prayed
Shook your mother's hand and slept

The message found us across Lukonkobe
Where Yanna slept earlier in the day

How fear disappears when you hear
That which you always feared to hear

(iv)

Yananda, mother of Luhlaba, my daughter
Do you sleep when our roof is blown off

Deborah, Masida, do not sleep now
Look at the scowling sky above us

Nellie, do you hear the wind howling
Irene, Fanny, Fulata, far far away

Who will lead the funeral dance, Ngcimezi
Who will lead the procession, Dumisa

When at last I walked into the bedroom
Growling and thundering in my stomach

Heralded such an incessant downpour
I feared my intestines would come out

(v)

To the west of Lukonkobe a gathering
At the home of Yanna, my boy's dream

I remember how she danced *twist*
And carried me to heights of Mparayi

I showed her father, Kasito, my cow
And helped her mother to reap millet

But Yanna displayed her beauty too early
And claws from all the winds tore at it

To the east of Lukonkobe the wind
Whispering in the trees belies the message

But the dry grass and harvested fields
Proclaim loud the passing of a season

(vi)

Elina Phakati, daughter of Uyanikhataza
You have fulfilled the vows you made

Vows are made in the depths of the heart
Not in the pomp of a church ceremony

Linley, Patricia, daughters who shed
The first tears when the flame blew out

Do not look for tears in my eyes
Before we plant him in the kraal

Before those staging their melodramas go
And those who come to practise proverbs

The last screw twisted into the Formica
Robbing us forever of his smiling face

(vii)

Luhlaba, son of Ndabambi, of Mwochwa
Listen when I call you by your name

A year has gone since you left us
And now fortitude deserts me

At night in the solitude of my room
Sleep drains out into silent tears

Your word was a poultice on my sores
Your word was a cudgel in your hand

The herdsman only shouts the name
And a wayward cow stops and turns

Now who is there to shout the name
And who will care to stop and turn

                    Mzuzu TTC, August 1989

Song of Sorrow
(Pacali patali pasirya pa nyanja)
(for Thom, Julian, Alice, Rose and
Fanny: Bana mwalekera njani?)

It's still far
It's still far across the river
     Lay the ropes
     For me to cross too

It's still far
It's still far across the lake
     Many have gone
     But no one has come back

It's still far
It's still far across time
     How can I sing
     And dance alone
     When my heart
     Is sinking in many a tear

Silence Returned

(i)

Machine of men
With fossil power
Puff slow, slow

Up the green hills;
For though the road be bumpy
And the engine loud

There's silence up the hills;
There's dryness
And the memory of rivers

Memory of cool pools
Where ripples
Deface all serenity

(ii)

Machine of men
Puff slow, slow
On the road to Madisi

For the yellow sun
Stares at us, crouched
Around whiteness.

This stripling
Went to school
But silence returns;

Only yesterday
Fully agile
Now, a cold presence

(iii)

Power of fossils
That rolls the world,
Push us gently

Along sandy tracks
Through farms and forest
To that forlorn hill.

Our heads reel
As questions search
The wilderness of knowledge:

Is beauty tinder
For burning youth;
Is love autolytic

(iv)

Machine of men
Squandering the treasure of fossils
Puff slow into Sungeni:

A huddle of huts
Below a gold-crowned hill.
Now the reality of sorrow:

Hearts of stone melt
As men shake their heads
In silent agony of sorrow;

And tears of children,
Of mothers and grandmothers
Erode all fortitude

Salima, Feb. 1978

(A secondary school boy was beaten to death by a village boy
who waylaid him as he escorted a primary school girl-friend of
his. There was an eclipse of the sun the day we took his body
to Sungeni, Madisi)

Solomoni Moyo
(for Fulata, Samson, Luthando and Chawezi)

Strolling across the fields after sunrise
The Gardener ties ribbons to flowers
Chosen to add colours to his trophies

Six weeks agony of cancer of the liver
Could not convince us you had to go
As we clung on praying Psalm 118:17

On 22nd April you pointed to the ceiling
And declared that you wanted to go home
Then in a beam of light you joined angels

At Daniel Gausi, Mzimba, your burial
Was a celebration of praise attended by
A blissful atmosphere of your presence

Although our hearts are so wrung out
We glorify God for His gift of 39 years
Of your life - a fragrance of love to us

Zomba CC, 1999

Pelluna
(for Chimwemwe, Vitu, Rumbani, Uchizi and Wongani)

Till January the 3rd, you walked the clay
Blissful, unruffled by wind, sun or rain

If you had died of an incurable somatic
Condition, we could have understood

Why did death waylay you near Thondwe
Steering the car to an ogrish blue-gum

Now Edrinnie and Benjamin are riddled
With fractures, lacerations and questions

Oh, some days are rotten, from sunrise
Some weeks must be thrown into the bin

They say crying can release the burden
Of sorrows and allow in some laughter

True there have been moments to cherish
But frequent tears often shroud sunshine

Pelluna, we yearn for your diamond faith
So we can see the way through mountains

Zomba CC, 2004

Pelluna Khoswe (nee Lora) died in a car accident near
Thondwe Village Polytechnic on 3rd January 2004. Her
husband, Benjamin, had cuts and bruises; and Pelluna's
sister, Dr. Edrinnie Kayambazinthu, had serious fractures
and cuts, which took many months to heal.

Fire on Dunduzu Hall
(for Kazinga and Yindole)

Yesterday
Restless tongues of fire, like
Tongues of the seven-headed dragon,
Rose on Dunduzu Hall

From everywhere
People came running
As if the Seven Trumpets
Had summoned them to come
And render their accounts

Tummies from the cafeteria
Pot-bellies, balds, brains
And spectacles, heeded
The rustic warning:
The last goat (to enter
The pen) shits with whips

Tongues rose
Like banners over a defeated fort;
While inside, the fire
Rumbled and devoured to ash
All that cost man
Years of toil and sweat

Submerged in smoke
Firemen battled with flames
While inmates scuttled
In and out of rooms
Moving their belongings
From the clutch of fire

A white fellow
Knew the mnemonic power
Of his small photo-box;

Calmly knelt, aiming
The very bowels of hell:
Then with precision
Pressing with his finger,
It went - click!

Kazinga braved the fire,
Leaping over tongues,
Sweeping our room clean
Of our luggage, before
The Dragon established
His dominion there

And Hebe was everywhere,
Working like a single hand
Combating a legion of fiends;
Yindole of Lukonkobe,
A veritable Ngoni warrior.

Hours of battle,
And the tongues sank
And the roaring bowels
Sizzled to smoke
And then ashes.

Dunduzu Hall (named after Dunduzu Chisiza,
a visionary politician during Malawi's independence,
who died in a mysterious road accident) was gutted
by fire, at Chancellor College, Zomba, Saturday,
25th October, 1975.

The Way
(Ndilongorani ntowa)

Show me the way
Show me the way

Show me, for I am tired
And I want to go to sleep

I took a little porridge
And now it moves in my eyes

Wherever I have to go
Across the river and the wild

The song I love to sing
Is show me the way

Song of the Mellow

We, with the Ngoni frailty
Shall quietly squeeze through

We, lovers of the calabash
Shall stealthily totter past

When the gates open wide
And saints go marching in

For adorers have forgotten
The water miracle of Cana

And the bearers of the gospel
Have sneaked back to Sodom

So we, the true worshippers
Shall sprinkle malt on the alter

To avert the brimstone anger
And fired up by the yodelling

And *hlombe* of the nubile nieces
Of our wives, singing our praises

Shall shift the earth with stamping
To raise a mighty oblation of dust

Dotolo of Ekwendeni

(A Dotolo nawo mwe)

People of Ekwendeni
And of areas around
Forget not Dotolo

His hair cut and combed
Leaving a straight ridge
Like a crest of white

Dotolo in the market
Patrolling, and no thief
No litterbug would dare

Dotolo down the street
Dancing classic malipenga
Like Soliyamu of Nkamanga

His shirt and short ironed
To razor-sharpness, his stick
Spinning like a fast wheel

Dotolololo-tolo, Dotolotolotolo
Dotolo rebuffs ticks
And ticks rebuff Dotolo

Then time for old English:
One deck you see the man
Is he coming? This means

When I called Nyaukandawire
She turned into an anthill,
Therefore Dotolo is a god

Children, we listened to him
The teacher from Nkamanga

Bewitched for his learning

He was our Ekwendeni
More than the Asian stores
Full of biscuits and sweets

But one day some men came
Saying he was their brother
And they were taking him

No one stopped our Dotolo going
Soon dusty word blew back from
The mound that swallowed Dotolo

Notes

Amakhosi balibele nokudhla, abayazi oluzayo,
princes are engrossed in feasting, they do not
know what is coming; a song Dr. Elmslie, the
early missionary at Ekwendeni, used to sing
with children at school.

A Morotoni, nyanga babika 'nkhokwe
(from a vimbuza song): Morotoni keeps
witchcraft horns (gourds etc) inside a granary.

A Dotolo nawo mwe.
a song children sang for Dotolo, a madman at
Ekwendeni in the 1960's

Bana (m)walekera njani
Literally, (addressing the dead) with whom
have you left the children? Means, who will
look after the children?

Boyi, a boy, servant.

Ciuta ndi linga lithu
Psalms 46: 1-2. In *Sumu za Ukhristu*
no. 150 and 152.

Dona, a white woman.

Epiphania Bonjesi,
a girl, shot by a policeman while she was
playing on the veranda of her aunt's house;
she died shortly after. The police invaded
Blantyre and other cities where people were
demonstrating after the elections.

Fanikiso Phiri
a 3rd year BEd student at Chancellor College,
University of Malawi, shot by the police
during a campus disorder, died 14th December,
2001.

Hagar
a woman who, with her child, was sent away
into the wilderness, Genesis 21.

Hinya

(from *inya*, for *yes* in Chitumbuka) is a derogatory term for northerners in Malawi.

Hlombe

is rhythmic clapping of hands by Ngoni women which accompanies Ingoma songs.

Inkosana

(diminutive of *inkosi*, king) In Mzimba there are different layers of traditional rulers: from *Inkosi-ya-makhosi* M'mbelwa, (literally King of kings) whose government designation is Paramount Chief; *Amakhosi*, such as *Inkosi* Mtwaro, designated Traditional Authority; *Amankosana*, such as *Inkosana* Lubinga Singini, who are in charge of an area, which could be more that 15 km in radius, eg. Inkosana Lazaro Jere extends from outside Ekwendeni, on the Mzuzu-Karonga road, to Luzi, near Phwezi; under these are Izinduna, village headmen, who are official advisors to rulers, even the King.

Jehu, a furious driver, from 2Kings 9:20.

Kaluphya, means (a small) wild fire

Lirani aMalawi, lirani

(based on a Catholic or Anglican hymn sang on funerals): Weep Malawians, weep.

Lukonkobe

Is a river, with its source at Choma mountain; it is prone to sudden flooding because of the high rainfall around Mzuzu.

Listonya:

W.J. Livingstone, a white manager of Bruce's estates, where *thangata* was practised.

Machona

(singular *muchona*) are people who go to work in far away land (eg South Africa) and come back old, or never come back.

Madang'ombe is Mumba's chieftain title.

Majure or Ndelerita are traditional wedding dances.

Mandazi is a kind of doughnut.

Matemvu
Clement, a finalist BEd student killed in a minibus while returning to college after forced closure after the police killed Fanikiso.

Matafale
a musician, detained because of a critical document he allegedly authored, died in police custody.

Matora
is public transport in vehicles not registered for passenger service.

Mgubo is a Ngoni dance celebrating victory.

Mparayi
a hill about 8 km from Ekwendeni; it looks like a bull facing south, seen from Engcongolweni village.

Mphini
beauty tattoos on a woman's' face, chest and thighs.

Msangu
(Acacia abide), a tree common along Malawi littoral. It sheds leaves during planting time for maize and puts forth new leaves towards harvesting time.

Munganya-muweme:
a good friend or person. When the leader of AFORD party was made 2nd Vice President, he said *Mang'anya uyu ndi mwema*, referring to the President as they addressed people in the North.

N. A. C:
Nyasaland African Congress, a party that preceded the Malawi Congress Party.

Ndilongorani ntowa
> from a song, means, show me the way.
> Ndimwe adada, ndimwe mama
> Ndiri mwana wino, adada
> Mleke kudinginyika, amama
> Ahee! nicali kupenja.

> Based on a song of a medicine man, Citikwira,
> which says:
> You my father, you my mother
> I am your son, father
> Do not complain, mother
> Look! I'm still searching

Ng'ombe, apa mukulira ng'ombe, nkayitorenku.
> a song my father liked to sing while playing a
> bango, a kind of zither; it is translated in the
> first stanza of 'Song of an Orphan'.

Nyavitima
> *Nya* is a title of respect for a woman,
> especially when married. *Vitima* means
> sorrows.

Omunaanga nchiyani
> a song from Dowa, means, my husband, what
> is this?

Ooo! Viphya, viphya wabazungu
translated in the first two lines of the poem.

Pakupoka wanangwa pali suzgo na viphyo
> lines from a song that says freedom comes
> after pain and suffering.

Paweme means goodbye or farewell.

Pelekani is time for giving gifts at a wedding
> ceremony

Poliro is a sound herdsboys pipe from their
> hands, to call others.

Sikusinja
> from a folktale of a secret murder reported by
> a singing bird.

Sidyabeni bobaba
    is a mgubo song, calling elders to celebrate
    their victory.
Sima
    a thick porridge, taken with relish such as okra
    or beef.
Tabakumwa moba, tam'phapatizga
    song the Ngoni, disciplined by the church
    because of drunkenness, sang, saying, they
    will squeeze through the gate of Heaven as the
    saints go in.
Thangata
    was a system practised by white farmers,
    whereby all black people who lived on their
    land had to give free labour.
Twist was a dancing style popular in the mid
    60's.
Umhlaba kaunoni
    is a Ngoni proverb that could be translated: the
    earth never gets fats (with many bodies buried
    in it.
Vwira
    is a spiritual force, more benevolent than
    Napolo, visualised in the form of a huge
    snake. On Nyika Plateau, Vwira punished
    anyone killing animals for gain.
Wamwana leka kulira, anyoko baya kudambo
    (A lullaby): Child stop crying, your mother
    has gone to the river (to draw water).
Yesu wane, wandicema, nkuruta... says, my
    Jesus has called me I am going...
Za-sin-tha! U-def, Boma!
    From a party slogan claiming that there is
    social and economic development since the
    party is the government.